Speak Logically 2

SPEECH TOPICS for KIDS

saramin

Introduction

Speak Logically: SPEECH TOPICS for KIDS was designed to teach young students the basic elements of public speaking and to prepare them to become confident English speakers. Students develop their speeches through vocabulary, listening, organizing, and speech writing exercises. Each unit includes a model speech and public speaking tips. Through regular practice and presentations, students improve public speaking skills and overall fluency.

Table of Contents

Unit Breakdown

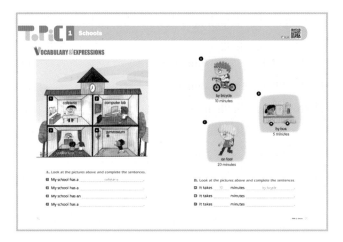

Introduce T.PiC

Students are presented with a new topic in each unit. They share personal experiences and opinions on a given topic with classmates through warm up questions and class discussions.

WHAT TO DO:

1 Ask one or two warm up questions to get students thinking about their personal experiences about the topic.

2 Have a brief classroom discussion to see how much students know and how well they are able to express themselves about the given topic.

VOCABULARY & EXPRESSIONS MP3

Students learn words and expressions related to the speech topic. The audio file allows them to listen to and practice the correct pronunciation of each word and expression.

WHAT TO DO:
1 Listen to vocabulary words on audio.
2 Go over any unfamiliar words, offer words with similar meanings, and provide more examples.
3 Ask students to come up with more words related to the speech topic.
4 Add the new words to the vocabulary list for future reference.

Students complete spelling, vocabulary, and grammar exercises in preparation for speech writing. Vocabulary Practice helps students become familiar with new vocabulary and see how it is used in a sentence.

WHAT TO DO:
1 Have students complete exercises and then take up answers.
2 Answers can be taken up as a class or in pairs.
   (Answers provided in Teachers' Guide.)

LISTENING PRACTICE MP3

Students are presented with a dialog between two to three people. They listen to the dialog and answer questions. When put in order, the answers become the model speech presented in the following section of the unit. In addition, Listening Practice demonstrates the logical sequence of the model speech: *Introductory statement – Reason - Example/Details - Closing Statement.*

WHAT TO DO:

1 Listen to the dialog and have students write out answers in full.
2 Listen to the dialog again so students can double check their answers.
3 Take up answers. (Answers provided in Teachers' Guide.)

MODEL SPEECH MP3

Students listen to a model speech and then practice reading the speech out loud alone or to a partner. They focus on pronouncing the words and listening to themselves speak. The model speech gives students an example of how a speech is written using words from the vocabulary list and how it sounds when spoken at the average speaking rate in a strong, confident voice.

WHAT TO DO:

1 Listen to the model speech.
2 Have students read it out loud three times either alone or in pairs.

BRAINSTORM

Students are presented with questions and/or graphic organizers. They learn to gather and organize information in preparation for speech writing. Students are encouraged to use vocabulary and expressions learned in the unit.

WHAT TO DO:

1 Read over questions, explain in detail what to do.
2 Have students fill in the graphic organizer and write out their answers.
3 If time permits, have students share their ideas with a partner.

SPEECH RITING

Students personalize a speech by filling in the blanks with information from their brainstorm. Each student completes their speech to practice and present to the class.

WHAT TO DO:

1 Have students fill in the blanks using information gathered in their brainstorm.
2 Once speeches are completed, they should look over their writing for any spelling or grammatical errors.
3 If time permits, have students work in pairs to read each other's speeches and check for any mistakes.

PRESENTATION

The Presentation section is divided into three sections. In section A, students write out their entire speech. In section B, students record their speeches and practice in front of a mirror. Students also practice a new public speaking skill in each unit such as using body language and their voices correctly. In section C, students complete a chart after presenting their speeches. The focus is on learning, practicing, and improving basic public speaking skills through each presentation, not on how perfectly each speech is delivered.

WHAT TO DO:

BEFORE PRESENTATIONS:

1 Have students write out the full speech.
2 Go over the steps to follow when practicing and give adequate time for practice.
3 Introduce the public speaking tip included in the Teachers' Guide.
4 If time permits, break the class into smaller groups or pairs for more practice.
5 Before starting presentations, go over any unfamiliar words in section C.

DURING PRESENTATIONS:

1 Make sure all students give their full attention to each speaker.
2 The goal is to have students thinking and speaking at the same time with minimal assistance. Students should be discouraged from using cue cards or reading their speeches from their textbooks. If a student gets stuck while presenting, provide a few words from their speech as hints so they can pick up from where they left off.

AFTER PRESENTATIONS:

1 Provide brief feedback and words of encouragement for each student immediately after his presentation. Feedback is most effective when given right after a

presentation as it will be fresh in the student's mind.

2   Classmates may also provide feedback to the presenter. Ask the class, "What is something the speaker did very well?", "What did you like about his speech?" Getting the class involved will encourage them to listen and watch their peers' presentations more attentively.

3   Each student should complete Section C immediately after their presentation.

➕ ADDITIONAL SUGGESTIONS

Set up a video camera in class to record students during presentations. Students get the chance to see what they look and sound like in front of an audience. It will also help them identify their strengths and weaknesses which they can further work on for the next presentation. Videos also help students feel more comfortable speaking in front of a camera. It may be fun for students to watch themselves on a classroom Youtube channel and to leave positive feedback for each other.

T.PiC 1 Schools

VOCABULARY & EXPRESSIONS

A. Look at the pictures above and complete the sentences.

1 My school has a ___cafeteria___ .

2 My school has a _____ .

3 My school has an _____ .

4 My school has a _____ .

by bicycle
10 minutes

by bus
5 minutes

on foot
20 minutes

B. Look at the pictures above and complete the sentences.

A It takes _____10_____ minutes _____by bicycle_____ .

B It takes _____ minutes _____ .

C It takes _____ minutes _____ .

 **ISTENING PRACTICE** 01_02

Listen and answer the questions using the sentences below.

> I go to Smith Elementary School in New York.
>
> It takes five minutes on foot.
>
> I like my school because it has a big jungle gym and auditorium.
>
> My school is close to my home.

1 What school do you go to?

_____

2 Is your school close to or far from your home?

_____

3 How long does it take to get to school?

_____

4 Why do you like your school?

_____

MODEL SPEECH

01_03

I go to Smith Elementary School in New York.

My school is close to my home.

It takes five minutes on foot.

I like my school because it has a big jungle gym

and auditorium.

PRACTICE
Out Loud!

BRAINSTORM

Answer questions about your school.

1. What school do you go to?

2. Where is it located? (city/district)

3. Is your school close to or far from your home?

4. How long does it take to get to school?

5. How do you get to school every day?
   ⓐ by bicycle   ⓑ by bus   ⓒ by car
   ⓓ on foot   ⓔ other: _____

6. Why do you like your school?

SPEECH WRITING

Use the words from your brainstorm to fill in the blanks.

I go to [_____] in [_____].

My school is [close to/far from] my home.

It takes [_____].

I like my school because [_____]

and [_____].

PRESENTATION

A **Write your entire speech below.**

⊙ Record

_____

_____

_____

_____

_____

_____

_____

B **Practice your speech in the following steps:**

STEP **1** Read your speech out loud.

STEP **2** Record your voice and listen to your speech.

STEP **3** Stand in front of a mirror and say your speech 3 times.
Try to remember the main points.

PRACTICE
Out Loud!

C **Present your speech. Have someone answer the questions.**

CRITERIA	Yes	No
1 The speaker stood up straight and tall.		
2 The speaker spoke loudly.		
3 The speaker made eye contact with the audience.		
4 The speaker looked confident.		

VOCABULARY & EXPRESSIONS

1

soccer

every day

2

baseball

once a week

3

golf

once a month

4

badminton

twice a week

5

ice hockey

twice a month

A. Unscramble the letters. Then write each word two times.

1 s l a l b b e a

_____ baseball _____   _____ baseball _____

2 f g l o

_____ _____

3 d a b i m n n t o

_____ _____

4 i e c o h c k y e

_____ _____

B. Look at the pictures and complete the sentences.

1 I play soccer _____ every day _____ .

2 I play baseball _____ a week.

3 I play golf _____ a month.

3 I play badminton _____ a week.

4 I play ice hockey _____ a month.

 ISTENING PRACTICE 🔊 02_02

Listen and answer the questions using the sentences below.

> I play soccer every day after school.
>
> It's a lot of fun because I play with my friends.
>
> Soccer is a great sport.

1 What sport do you like to play?

_____

2 How often do you play?

_____

3 Why is it fun?

_____

4 Playing sports is good for your health!

MODEL SPEECH

02_03

Listen to the speech and then read it out loud three times.

Soccer is a great sport.

I play soccer every day after school.

It's a lot of fun because I play with my friends.

Playing sports is good for your health!

PRACTICE
Out Loud!

BRAINSTORM

Answer questions about your favorite sport.

1. What sport do you like to play?

2. Why is this sport fun?

3. How often do you play this sport? Choose one answer or write your own.

   ⓐ every day   ⓑ once a week   ⓒ twice a week

   ⓓ once a month   ⓔ twice a month

   ⓕ other:

SPEECH WRITING

Use the words from your brainstorm to fill in the blanks.

_____ is a great sport.

I play _____ .

It's a lot of fun because _____ .

Playing sports is good for your health!

PRESENTATION

A **Write your entire speech below.** ⊙ Record

_____

_____

_____

_____

_____

_____

_____

B **Practice your speech in the following steps:**

STEP **1** Read your speech out loud.

STEP **2** Record your voice and listen to your speech.

STEP **3** Stand in front of a mirror and say your speech 3 times.
Try to remember the main points.

PRACTICE
Out Loud!

C **Present your speech. Have someone answer the questions.**

CRITERIA	Yes	No
1 The speaker stood up straight and tall.		
2 The speaker spoke loudly.		
3 The speaker made eye contact with the audience.		
4 The speaker looked confident.		

VOCABULARY & EXPRESSIONS

spring

summer

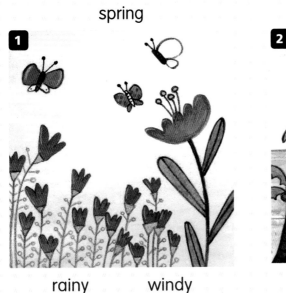

rainy   windy   hot   humid

A. Look at the pictures and complete each sentence.

1 My favorite season is _____.

2 My favorite season is _____.

3 My favorite season is _____.

4 My favorite season is _____.

fall

winter

sunny   cool

snowy   cold

B. Fill in the blanks to describe the weather for each season.

1 It is ___rainy___ and ___windy___ in the spring.

2 It is _____ and _____ in the summer.

3 It is _____ and _____ in the fall.

4 It is _____ and _____ in the winter.

 **LISTENING PRACTICE**

03_02

Listen and answer the questions using the sentences below.

It's great because the weather is sunny and cool.

Mine is the fall.

In the fall, I go hiking in the mountains.

1 What is your favorite season?

_____

2 What do you do during this season?

_____

3 How is the weather during your favorite season?

_____

MODEL SPEECH

Listen to the speech and then read it out loud three times.

What is your favorite season?

Mine is the fall.

In the fall, I go hiking in the mountains.

It's great because the weather is sunny and cool.

PRACTICE
Out Loud!

BRAINSTORM

Write words that describe your favorite season.

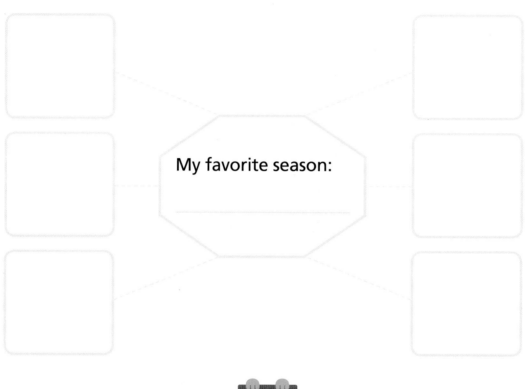

My favorite season:

_____

SPEECH WRITING

Use the words from your brainstorm to fill in the blanks.

What is your favorite season?

Mine is the [ ] .

In the [ ] , I [ ] .

It's great because the weather is [ ]

and [ ] .

PRESENTATION

A **Write your entire speech below.**

⊙ Record

_____

_____

_____

_____

_____

_____

B **Practice your speech in the following steps:**

STEP 1 Read your speech out loud.

STEP 2 Record your voice and listen to your speech.

STEP 3 Stand in front of a mirror and say your speech 3 times. Try to remember the main points.

PRACTICE
Out Loud!

C **Present your speech. Have someone answer the questions.**

CRITERIA	Yes	No
1 The speaker stood up straight and tall.		
2 The speaker spoke loudly.		
3 The speaker made eye contact with the audience.		
4 The speaker looked confident.		

VOCABULARY & EXPRESSIONS

1

music teacher

2

math teacher

3

science teacher

A. Look at the pictures above and complete the sentences.

1 She is my   music teacher   .

2 She is my   .

3 She is my   .

English teacher

P.E. teacher

history teacher

B. Look at the pictures above and complete the sentences.

A He is my _English teacher_ .

B He is my _____ .

C He is my _____ .

Listen and answer the questions using the sentences below.

> Her classes are always interesting.
>
> Ms. Park is the best teacher.
>
> She is my fourth grade music teacher.

1 Who is your favorite teacher?

_____

2 Who is she?

_____

3 How would you describe her classes?

_____

4 I hope to have more teachers like Ms. Park in the future!

Listen to the speech and then read it out loud three times.

Ms. Park is the best teacher.

She is my fourth grade music teacher.

Her classes are always interesting.

I hope to have more teachers like Ms. Park in the

future!

BRAINSTORM

Answer questions about your favorite teacher.

1. Who is your favorite teacher?

2. For which grade and subject were you in his/her class?

3. Write two words that describe his/her classes.

SPEECH WRITING

Use the words from your brainstorm to fill in the blanks.

_____ is the best teacher.

He/She   is/was   my   _____ grade

_____ teacher.

His/Her   classes   are/were   always   _____ .

I hope to have more teachers like _____

in the future!

PRESENTATION

A **Write your entire speech below.**

⊙ Record

_____

_____

_____

_____

_____

_____

B **Practice your speech in the following steps:**

STEP **1** Read your speech out loud.

STEP **2** Record your voice and listen to your speech.

STEP **3** Stand in front of a mirror and say your speech 3 times.
Try to remember the main points.

PRACTICE
Out Loud!

C **Present your speech. Have someone answer the questions.**

CRITERIA	Yes	No
1 The speaker stood up straight and tall.		
2 The speaker spoke loudly.		
3 The speaker made eye contact with the audience.		
4 The speaker looked confident.		

VOCABULARY & EXPRESSIONS

A. Label the different areas of the neighborhood.

 1 c _____

 2 p _____

 3 r _____

 4 a _____

B. Fill in the blanks to complete the sentences.

1 The park is _____peaceful_____ .

2 The apartment is _____ .

3 The playground is _____ .

4 The restaurant is _____ .

5 The community center is _____ .

 **ISTENING PRACTICE** 05_02

Listen and answer the questions using the sentences below.

> We also swim at the community center.
>
> My friends and I hang out at the playground.
>
> There are a lot of apartments and restaurants.

1 My neighborhood is very busy.

2 Describe your neighborhood. What does it look like?

3 Where do you usually hang out with your friends?

4 What else do you do with your friends?

Listen to the speech and then read it out loud three times.

My neighborhood is very busy.

There are a lot of apartments and restaurants.

My friends and I hang out at the playground.

We also swim at the community center.

PRACTICE
Out Loud!

BRAINSTORM

Answer questions about your neighborhood.

1. Write a word that best describes your neighborhood.

2. What does it look like?

3. Where do you usually hang out with your friends?

4. What else do you do with your friends?

SPEECH WRITING

Use the words from your brainstorm to fill in the blanks.

My neighborhood is _____ .

There are _____ .

My friends and I hang out at _____ .

We also _____ .

RESENTATION

A **Write your entire speech below.**   ⦿ Record

_____

_____

_____

_____

_____

_____

_____

B **Practice your speech in the following steps:**

STEP **1** Read your speech out loud.

STEP **2** Record your voice and listen to your speech.

STEP **3** Stand in front of a mirror and say your speech 3 times.
Try to remember the main points.

PRACTICE
Out Loud!

C **Present your speech. Have someone answer the questions.**

CRITERIA	Yes	No
1 The speaker stood up straight and tall.		
2 The speaker spoke loudly.		
3 The speaker made eye contact with the audience.		
4 The speaker looked confident.		

VOCABULARY & EXPRESSIONS

1

classical

2

hip hop

3

pop

4

rock

A. Look at the pictures above and complete the sentences.

1 I love listening to _____classical_____ music.

2 I love listening to _____ music.

3 I love listening to _____ music.

4 I love listening to _____ music.

cheerful

energetic

wonderful

relaxed

B. Draw a line between adjectives that have a similar meaning.

1 cheerful •   • calm

2 relaxed •   • great

3 wonderful •   • happy

4 energetic •   • active

 **L**ISTENING PRACTICE 06_02

Listen and answer the questions using the sentences below.

> I listen to music in the car and before going to bed.
>
> I love listening to classical music.
>
> Classical music makes me feel relaxed and calm.
>
> My favorite composer is Mozart.

1 What type of music do you like listening to?

_____

2 Who is your favorite composer?

_____

3 When do you listen to music?

_____

4 How does it make you feel?

_____

Listen to the speech and then read it out loud three times.

I love listening to classical music.

My favorite composer is Mozart.

I listen to music in the car and before going to bed.

Classical music makes me feel relaxed and calm.

BRAINSTORM

Answer questions about your favorite type of music.

1. WHAT?
   (What type of music do you like?)

2. WHO?
   (Who is your favorite singer, band, or composer?)

3. WHEN?
   (When do you listen to music?)

4. HOW?
   (How does it make you feel?)

SPEECH WRITING

Use the words from your brainstorm to fill in the blanks.

I love listening to _____ .

My favorite _____ is _____ .

I listen to music _____ .

_____ makes me feel _____ .

PRESENTATION

A **Write your entire speech below.** ⊙ Record

_____

_____

_____

_____

_____

_____

_____

B **Practice your speech in the following steps:**

STEP **1** Read your speech out loud.

STEP **2** Record your voice and listen to your speech.

STEP **3** Stand in front of a mirror and say your speech 3 times. Try to remember the main points.

PRACTICE Out Loud!

C **Present your speech. Have someone answer the questions.**

CRITERIA	Yes	No
1 The speaker stood up straight and tall.		
2 The speaker spoke loudly.		
3 The speaker made eye contact with the audience.		
4 The speaker looked confident.		

VOCABULARY & EXPRESSIONS

Drama

NEWS

Documentary

Sitcom

Movie

Sports

game show

A. Draw a line between each picture and the correct TV genre.

1

• movie

2

• game show

3

• sports

B. Write the plural form of each TV genre to complete the sentence.

1 I enjoy watching _____Sitcoms_____. (sitcom)

2 I enjoy watching _____. (drama)

3 I enjoy watching _____. (game show)

4 I enjoy watching _____. (documentary)

*(*news and sports do not require a plural form. documentary = documentaries)*

 **ISTENING PRACTICE**

07_02

Listen and answer the questions using the sentences below.

> This show makes me want to study harder.
>
> It's a great show to watch with my family.
>
> I enjoy watching game shows on television.
>
> These days, I watch Golden Bell Challenge.

1 What type of TV shows do you like watching?

_____

2 What do you watch these days?

_____

3 Why do you like this show?

_____

4 Who do you watch this show with?

_____

MODEL SPEECH

Listen to the speech and then read it out loud three times.

I enjoy watching game shows on television.

These days, I watch Golden Bell Challenge.

This show makes me want to study harder.

It's a great show to watch with my family.

PRACTICE
Out Loud!

BRAINSTORM

Answer questions about your favorite TV show.

1. What type of TV shows do you like watching?

2. What do you watch these days?

3. Why do you like this show?

4. Who do you watch this show with?

SPEECH WRITING

Use the words from your brainstorm to fill in the blanks.

I enjoy watching _____ on television.

These days, I watch _____ .

This show _____ .

It's a great show to watch _____ .

PRESENTATION

A **Write your entire speech below.**

....

....

....

....

....

....

B **Practice your speech in the following steps:**

STEP **1** Read your speech out loud.

STEP **2** Record your voice and listen to your speech.

STEP **3** Stand in front of a mirror and say your speech 3 times.
Try to remember the main points.

PRACTICE
Out Loud!

C **Present your speech. Have someone answer the questions.**

CRITERIA	Yes	No
1 The speaker stood up straight and tall.		
2 The speaker spoke loudly.		
3 The speaker made eye contact with the audience.		
4 The speaker looked confident.		

VOCABULARY & EXPRESSIONS

1 library

2 church

3 mall

4 community center

A. Look at the picture above and complete the sentences.

1 The _____library_____ is a great place to visit.

2 The _____ is a great place to visit.

3 The _____ is a great place to visit.

4 The _____ is a great place to visit.

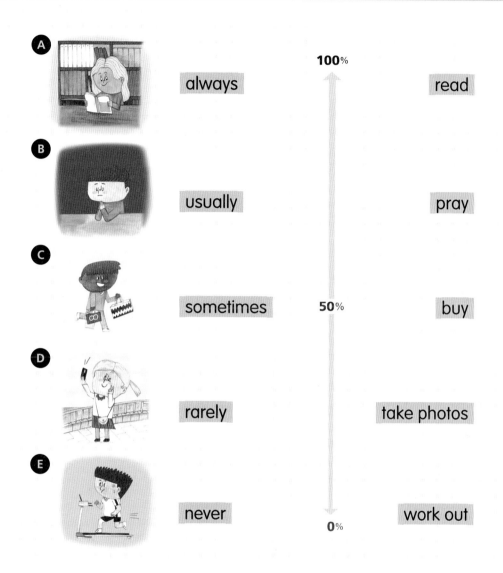

A	always	100% read
B	usually	pray
C	sometimes	50% buy
D	rarely	take photos
E	never	0% work out

B. Fill in the blanks with adverbs of frequency.

1. I _____*always*_____ read books.

2. I _____ pray for my family.

3. I _____ buy clothes.

4. I _____ take photos.

 **ISTENING PRACTICE** 08_02

Listen and answer the questions using the sentences below.

> I visit the library once a week.
>
> I like spending time there because it is very quiet.
>
> I usually read books and do my homework.
>
> The library is a great place to visit.

1 Where do you like to visit?

_____

2 How often do you go there?

_____

3 Why do you like spending time there?

_____

4 What do you do there?

_____

MODEL SPEECH

08_03

Listen to the speech and then read it out loud three times.

The library is a great place to visit.

I visit the library once a week.

I like spending time there because it is very quiet.

I usually read books and do my homework.

PRACTICE
Out Loud!

BRAINSTORM

Answer questions about a place you like to visit.

1. Where do you like to visit?

2. How often do you go there?

3. Why do you like spending time there?

4. What are two things you do there?

SPEECH WRITING

Use the words from your brainstorm to fill in the blanks.

_____ is a great place to visit.

I visit _____ .

I like spending time there because _____ .

I usually/sometimes/always _____ .

60

PRESENTATION

A **Write your entire speech below.**

⊙ Record

_____

_____

_____

_____

_____

_____

B **Practice your speech in the following steps:**

STEP **1** Read your speech out loud.

STEP **2** Record your voice and listen to your speech.

STEP **3** Stand in front of a mirror and say your speech 3 times.
Try to remember the main points.

PRACTICE
Out Loud!

C **Present your speech. Have someone answer the questions.**

CRITERIA	Yes	No
1 The speaker stood up straight and tall.		
2 The speaker spoke loudly.		
3 The speaker made eye contact with the audience.		
4 The speaker looked confident.		

VOCABULARY & EXPRESSIONS

1

swimmer

Athletes

2

figure skater

3

runner

A. Look at the pictures above and complete the sentences.

1 He is a popular _____Swimmer_____.

2 She is a popular _____.

3 He is a popular _____.

courageous

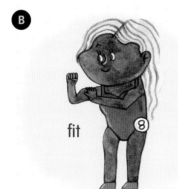

fit

popular

B. Draw a line between words that have a similar meaning.

1 popular • • healthy

2 courageous •————————• brave

3 fit • • famous

 **ISTENING PRACTICE**

09_02

Listen and answer the questions using the sentences below.

> I admire her because she practices very hard and always tries her best.
>
> The athlete I admire most is Yuna Kim.
>
> She is a popular Korean figure skater.
>
> Yuna Kim won a gold medal at the 2010 Winter Olympics.

1 Which athlete do you admire most?

_____

2 Who is she?

_____

3 Why do you admire her?

_____

4 What interesting fact do you know about her?

_____

*try one's best/do one's best = to try very hard

MODEL SPEECH

09_03

Listen to the speech and then read it out loud three times.

The athlete I admire most is Yuna Kim.

She is a popular Korean figure skater.

I admire her because she practices very hard and always tries her best.

PRACTICE
Out Loud!

Yuna Kim won a gold medal at the 2010 Winter Olympics.

BRAINSTORM

Answer questions about your favorite athlete.

1. Which athlete do you admire most?

2. a) What country is this athlete from?

   b) What sport does this athlete play?

3. Why do you admire this athlete?

4. What interesting fact(s) do you know about this athlete?

SPEECH WRITING

Use the words from your brainstorm to fill in the blanks.

The athlete I admire most is _____ .

He/She is a popular _____ _____ .

I admire him/her because _____ .

_____ .

PRESENTATION

A **Write your entire speech below.**

⊙ Record

_____

_____

_____

_____

_____

_____

_____

B **Practice your speech in the following steps:**

STEP **1** Read your speech out loud.

STEP **2** Record your voice and listen to your speech.

STEP **3** Stand in front of a mirror and say your speech 3 times.
Try to remember the main points.

PRACTICE Out **Loud!**

C **Present your speech. Have someone answer the questions.**

CRITERIA	Yes	No
1 The speaker stood up straight and tall.		
2 The speaker spoke loudly.		
3 The speaker made eye contact with the audience.		
4 The speaker looked confident.		

VOCABULARY & EXPRESSIONS

1

math - easy

2

art - fun

A. Draw a line between each subject and the correct description.

1 math •   • draw and paint

2 art •   • learn about the world
                                 around us

3 history •   • learn about past events

4 social studies •   • learn about numbers

3

history - boring

4

social studies - difficult

B. Look at the pictures and complete sentences.

1 Math is _____ easy _____.

2 Art is _____.

3 History is _____.

4 Social studies is _____.

 **ISTENING PRACTICE**

🔲 10_02

Listen and answer the questions using the sentences below.

> Math is fun because I like solving problems.
>
> A subject I dislike is history.
>
> I dislike history because there are many dates to remember.
>
> Math is my favorite subject in school.

1 What is your favorite subject in school?

_____

2 Why do you like it?

_____

3 What subject do you dislike?

_____

4 Why do you dislike this subject?

_____

MODEL SPEECH

10_03

Listen to the speech and then read it out loud three times.

Math is my favorite subject in school.

Math is fun because I like solving problems.

A subject I dislike is history.

I dislike history because there are many dates to remember.

PRACTICE
Out Loud!
1
2
3

BRAINSTORM

Answer questions about your favorite and least favorite subjects.

1. What is your favorite subject in school?

2. Why do you like this subject?

3. What subject do you dislike?

4. Why do you dislike this subject?

SPEECH WRITING

Use the words from your brainstorm to fill in the blanks.

[   ] is my favorite subject in school.

[   ] is fun because [   ].

A subject I dislike is [   ].

I dislike [   ] because [   ].

PRESENTATION

A **Write your entire speech below.**   ⊙ Record

_____

_____

_____

_____

_____

B **Practice your speech in the following steps:**

STEP **1** Read your speech out loud.

STEP **2** Record your voice and listen to your speech.

STEP **3** Stand in front of a mirror and say your speech 3 times.
Try to remember the main points.

PRACTICE
Out Loud!

C **Present your speech. Have someone answer the questions.**

CRITERIA	Yes	No
1 The speaker stood up straight and tall.		
2 The speaker spoke loudly.		
3 The speaker made eye contact with the audience.		
4 The speaker looked confident.		

VOCABULARY & EXPRESSIONS

I'm afraid of...

1 roller coasters

4 insects

2 snakes

3 ghosts

A. Look at the pictures above and complete the sentences.

1 I am afraid of _____roller coasters_____ .

2 I am afraid of _____ .

3 I am afraid of _____ .

4 I am afraid of _____ .

too fast

disgusting

Reasons

bite

scary

B. Look at the pictures above and complete the sentences.

1 I dislike snakes because they ___bite___ .

2 I dislike ghosts because they are _____ .

3 I dislike roller coasters because they are _____ .

4 I dislike insects because they are _____ .

 **ISTENING PRACTICE**

11_02

Listen and answer the questions using the sentences below.

> When I feel scared, I close my eyes and scream.
>
> I dislike snakes because they bite.
>
> I'm afraid of snakes.

1 What is your biggest fear?

_____

2 Why do you dislike them?

_____

3 What do you do when you feel scared?

_____

MODEL SPEECH

11_03

Listen to the speech and then read it out loud three times.

What is your biggest fear?

I'm afraid of snakes.

I dislike snakes because they bite.

When I feel scared, I close my eyes and scream.

PRACTICE
Out Loud!

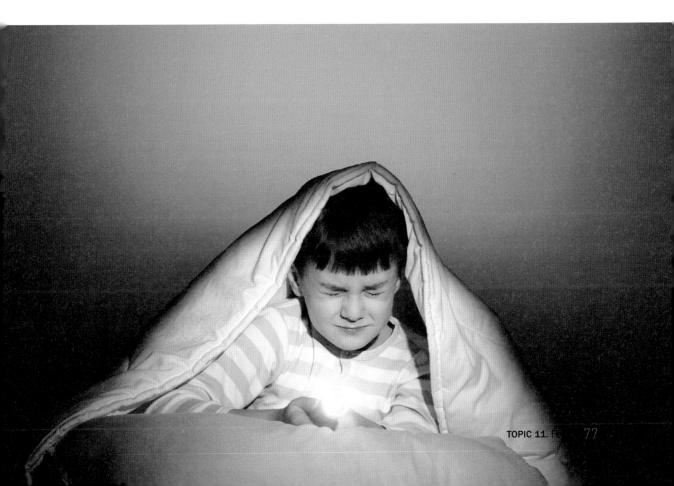

BRAINSTORM

Answer questions about what you are your worst fear.

1. What is your biggest fear?

2. Why do you dislike it/them?

3. What do you do when you feel scared?

SPEECH WRITING

Use the words from your brainstorm to fill in the blanks.

What is your biggest fear?

I'm afraid of [   ].

I dislike [   ] because [   ].

When I feel scared, I [   ].

PRESENTATION

A Write your entire speech below.   ⦿ Record

_____

_____

_____

_____

_____

_____

B Practice your speech in the following steps:

STEP **1** Read your speech out loud.

STEP **2** Record your voice and listen to your speech.

STEP **3** Stand in front of a mirror and say your speech 3 times.
Try to remember the main points.

PRACTICE
Out Loud!

C Present your speech. Have someone answer the questions.

CRITERIA	Yes	No
1 The speaker stood up straight and tall.		
2 The speaker spoke loudly.		
3 The speaker made eye contact with the audience.		
4 The speaker looked confident.		

12 Prized possessions

VOCABULARY & EXPRESSIONS

1

camera

2

diary

3
pet

4
toy

A. Look at the pictures above and complete the sentences.

1 This _____camera_____ is very special to me.

2 This _____ is very special to me.

3 This _____ is very special to me.

4 This _____ is very special to me.

prized possessions

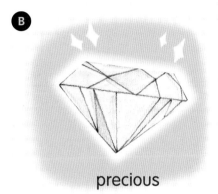

precious

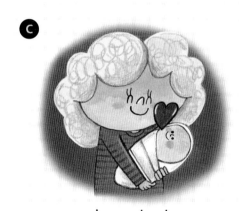

important

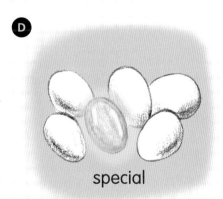

special

B. Look at the pictures above and complete the sentences.

A These jewels are my _____prized possessions_____ .

B A diamond is very _____ .

C A baby is very _____ to its mother.

D A golden egg is very _____ .

 **ISTENING PRACTICE** 🔲 12_02

Listen and answer the questions using the sentences below.

> It's special because my grandfather gave it to me.
>
> This camera is very special to me.
>
> I use it to take pictures of my family and friends.

1 What is your most prized possession?

_____

2 Why is it special?

_____

3 How or when do you use it?

_____

4 I hope to keep it forever!

MODEL SPEECH

12_03

Listen to the speech and then read it out loud three times.

This camera is very special to me.

It's special because my grandfather gave it to me.

I use it to take pictures of my family and friends.

I hope to keep it forever!

PRACTICE
Out Loud!

1
2
3

TOPIC 12. Prized possessions

BRAINSTORM

**Answer questions about your most prized possession.
Be prepared to bring it and show it to the class.**

1. What is your most prized possession?

2. Why is it your most prized possession?

3. How or when do you use it?

SPEECH WRITING

Use the words from your brainstorm to fill in the blanks.

This ⟨_____⟩ is

⟨very special / important / precious⟩ to me.

It's ⟨special / important / precious⟩

because ⟨_____⟩.

I use it ⟨_____⟩.

I hope to keep it forever!

PRESENTATION

A Write your entire speech below.

◉ Record

_____

_____

_____

_____

_____

_____

_____

B Practice your speech in the following steps:

STEP **1** Read your speech out loud.

STEP **2** Record your voice and listen to your speech.

STEP **3** Stand in front of a mirror and say your speech 3 times.
Try to remember the main points.

PRACTICE
Out Loud!

C Present your speech. Have someone answer the questions.

CRITERIA	Yes	No
1 The speaker stood up straight and tall.		
2 The speaker spoke loudly.		
3 The speaker made eye contact with the audience.		
4 The speaker looked confident.